HOW TO BE A DJ

IN 10 EASY LESSONS

DJ BOOMA

Walter Foster Jr.

ABOUT THE AUTHOR

DJ Booma (aka David Duncan) is a professional DJ and music producer from Leeds, UK. Booma started DJing and making music as a hobby when he was a child and he loved it so much he made it his career. Booma is also a professional dance teacher and teaches dance around the world. He leads international youth projects and is passionate about getting young people involved in the arts.

First Published in the UK in 2017 by QED Publishing
Part of The Quarto Group
The Old Brewery, 6 Blundell Street, London N7 9BH

Publisher: Maxime Boucknooghe
Art Director: Susi Martin
Editorial Director: Laura Knowles
Editor: Ellie Brough
Design: Claire Barber
Original Illustrations: Joanna Kerr

Published in the USA in 2017 by Walter Foster Jr.,
an imprint of The Quarto Group.
6 Orchard Road, Suite 100, Lake Forest, CA 92630, USA.
T (949) 380-7510 F (949) 380-7575 www.QuartoKnows.com

Walter Foster Jr. titles are also available at discount for retail, wholesale, promotional, and bulk purchase. For details, contact the Special Sales Manager by email at specialsales@quarto.com or by mail at The Quarto Group, Attn: Special Sales Manager, 401 Second Avenue North, Suite 310, Minneapolis, MN 55401 USA.

ISBN: 978 1 63322 398 1

Printed in China
10 9 8 7 6 5 4 3 2 1

MIX
Paper from responsible sources
FSC® C016973
FSC
www.fsc.org

CONTENTS

INTRODUCTION - 4

SUPER SKILL 1: UNDERSTANDING DJING - - - - - - - - - - - - - - 6

SUPER SKILL 2: MASTERING YOUR TOOLS - - - - - - - - - - - - - 10

SUPER SKILL 3: FEELING THE BEAT! - - - - - - - - - - - - - - - - 16

SUPER SKILL 4: MIXING IT UP - 22

SUPER SKILL 5: SCRATCHING - 28

SUPER SKILL 6: PRACTICE MAKES PERFECT - - - - - - - - - - - 34

SUPER SKILL 7: PREPARING A DJ SET - - - - - - - - - - - - - - - 38

SUPER SKILL 8: RECORDING YOUR SET - - - - - - - - - - - - - - 44

SUPER SKILL 9: PRODUCING A DEMO - - - - - - - - - - - - - - - 50

SUPER SKILL 10: PLAYING LIVE - - - - - - - - - - - - - - - - - - - 56

USEFUL LINKS - 62

GLOSSARY - 63

INDEX - 64

WELCOME TO THE WORLD OF DJING

DJing is amazing! The best DJs travel all around the world to play music in incredible places. You'll find DJs working in many exciting venues such as parties, fashion shows, and festivals. It's a fantastic career, but it can also be a super hobby. Reading this book is your first step on your DJ journey, whether you want to be a worldwide superstar or a bedroom mixer.

WHAT YOU WILL LEARN

In this book you'll find out how amazing DJing is— and how easy and fun it is to learn the key skills every great DJ must know. The ten easy lessons in this book will teach you how to be a DJ. Everything you need to know is right here, including how to mix music together, what equipment you can use, and how you can record your own DJ mixes to share. You may want to release them into the world as a demo, or perform them in front of a live audience!

WHAT YOU WILL NEED

A love of music and some enthusiasm will go a long way to making you a great DJ, but there are a few other tools you need before you get started. There are two main routes you can choose to take: the hardware-based route and the software-based route. Both routes require different equipment but will have a mix of both hardware and software elements.

DJs MAKE THE
WORLD A
HAPPIER PLACE!

DJ hardware that you will need:

- A pair of CD or vinyl decks (pages 10-11)
- A DJ mixer (page 12)
- A pair of active speakers (page 12)
- Headphones (page 12)
- Cables to connect all the equipment together (the types of cables will vary depending on the equipment you use)

AS A DJ, YOUR JOB IS TO CONNECT WITH PEOPLE THROUGH THE MUSIC YOU PLAY. DJS HAVE THE POWER TO MAKE PEOPLE FEEL DIFFERENT EMOTIONS AND MAKE THEM **DANCE, SING,** AND **BE HAPPY!**

DJ software that you will need:

- A laptop with at least two USB inputs
- DJ software/program (pages 12-13)
- DJ controller (page 13)
- A pair of active speakers
- An external sound card (page 13)
- Cables to connect all the equipment together (again, the types of cables you need will depend on your setup)

HANDY TIP!
Be unique! The best way to connect with your audience is to be yourself, so have fun and enjoy the music!

UNDERSTANDING DJING

Have you ever wondered how DJing first started? Or maybe you've never known exactly what the letters "DJ" stand for? In this chapter you'll learn some of the main tools, words, and phrases that DJs use. You will begin to understand the basics and this will give you a good starting point to grow and develop your own DJ skills!

HOW DID DJS BEGIN?

DJing roots are linked to the development of hip-hop music in the Bronx in New York City. In those days, the DJ's job was to "spin" popular records that kept people dancing and kept the party alive.

THE FIRST DJ

A man called DJ Kool Herc was the first person to be called a DJ. He originally came from Jamaica and moved to New York City, in the early 1970s. With no other DJs to learn from, he taught himself, just like many DJs do today!

DJ Kool Herc found that if he took two turntables (record players) and put them together with a "mixer" between them, he could then play two records or songs together. This became known as **turntablism**, and it let him continuously play music without any gaps for as long as he wanted. This is also what we call **mixing music together**.

DJs WORLDWIDE

Inspired by DJ Kool Herc, DJing spread around the world. In the UK it started to become a big movement from the early 1980s, developing mainly in the clubs or discos—as well as on early pioneering radio stations such as Radio 1. These stations helped to spread the new sounds of electro dance music, along with new DJs such as Carl Cox and Pete Tong. Some of these DJs became famous through playing and bringing exciting music to new audiences.

HANDY TIP!

A great way to find out more about DJs is to see them performing live. You can watch YouTube clips or music videos of DJs. You can also go to gigs and parties, but you need to make sure you have your parents' permission first!

THE DJs' DECK OF CHOICE

The Technics 1210 quickly became the **deck** of choice for many DJs. These decks are really important to the whole DJ culture because they are considered to be the best DJ turntable decks ever made. They have very strong direct drive turntables and are designed especially for DJing. You will learn all about their special features, because all modern DJ equipment follows the same specifications.

WHAT'S IN A NAME?

DJ is short for **disc jockey**. The meaning of the "disc" part is obvious, because a disc is the record or vinyl that contains recorded music! The "jockey" part is a bit more obscure. A jockey is a person who rides a horse in a race. One theory for why it is used in this context is that a radio DJ would play a song all the way through to the end, just like a jockey rides a horse all the way to the end of a race. Today's DJs are people who play music at parties, on the radio, in clubs, at special events, and more. Many DJs also make, produce, and play their own records!

HOW TO START

Deciding to become a DJ is the first step. Now you need to learn some techniques and build up your skills. Remember that anyone can be a DJ, including you—and most DJs start off DJing in their bedrooms as a hobby.

Tip 1: LISTEN TO OTHER DJS

Watch and listen to other DJs. Do you already have a favorite DJ? This will help give you some ideas on what style you like. If you like talking, maybe you could be a radio DJ, but if you like listening and dancing, maybe you could be a DJ who plays at parties.

Tip 2: BUILD UP A MUSIC COLLECTION

You will need to create and build up your own collection of music that you like. They can be mp3 files, wav files, or CDs. Many DJs think that old-fashioned vinyl records are actually the best format!

Tip 3: USE THE INTERNET

Online sites such as YouTube and other specialist DJ music sites are a great resource. You can find many different types of DJs, tutorials and videos of DJing, as well as lots of good music.

Tip 4: PRACTICE MAKES PERFECT!

The more you practice and learn about DJing, the better you will become, so do as much research as you can. Taking lessons is also a great way to learn. You can find tutorials online and look for DJ courses at local youth community centers, schools, and colleges.

HANDY TIP!

Listen to music on the radio, find out what kind of music you like, and watch and learn from other DJs.

TYPES OF DJS

There are many types of DJs, and each have their own specialties. Here are some of the main ones.

HIP-HOP DJ

A hip-hop DJ specializes in playing hip-hop and rap music. These are often referred to as urban forms of music. Hip-hop and rap are very much a lifestyle and image, with the music being a part of that.

HOUSE DJ

A house DJ specializes in playing house music, often called dance or electronic music. House music began when DJs began to create a type of dance music that was repetitive and hypnotic, which made it easy for people to dance to. Many house DJs also produce their own dance tracks and remixes.

RADIO DJ

Radio DJs play their own shows on the radio. Many also do gigs and festivals as well, and some become household names. These DJs work on commercial radio stations, internet radio stations, and underground stations.

CLUB DJ

A club DJ works mainly in nightclubs, but they often travel the world to play shows at festivals and music events. Many club DJs specialize in a particular style of music, but some play multi-style sets.

REMIXER

DJs also work as remixers, remaking music for other artists. This means taking an existing song and then making a new mix out of it. For example, they might add new sounds like a strong dance beat.

MASTERING YOUR TOOLS

The next step is learning about the tools a DJ uses; what they're called, what they do, and how to use them. Once you've learned the basics, you can see what works best for you. There are several different DJ setup options you can choose, but remember, no matter what equipment you use, it's all about being creative and inventive.

CD DECKS

CD decks allow you to DJ using CDs. The advantage of using CDs is that they are much smaller and lighter than vinyl records, yet can hold much more music. CD decks are like vinyl decks and have the same basic features, but because they are digital, you can do more things with them. They range from entry-level decks up to professional ones.

HANDY TIP!
Whatever equipment you choose, they all have similar features so you can transfer your skills easily once you learn the basics!

CD deck features

TRACK SEARCH
allows you to search tracks on a CD

DISPLAY
tells you important information: the track number, track time, and pitch value

CUE BUTTON
saves the track position so you can cue it to the mix later

PLAY/PAUSE
allows you to play and pause the track

JOG WHEEL
speeds up or slows down a track

RPM IS THE NUMBER OF REVOLUTIONS OR SPINS A RECORD TURNS PER MINUTE.

PITCH CONTROL
alters the speed or sound of the record so that you can get two records to play together at the same speed

RECORD VINYL DECKS

Vinyl decks or **turntables** are used for playing records or vinyl. A pair of beginner's decks is the best option when you are starting out. They will most likely be belt-driven (meaning the motor is driven by a rubber belt). You can also get direct-drive versions, which are better to use because they are driven by a strong magnet, making the deck more responsive and easier to mix and scratch on.

VINYL

Vinyl records are analog and have two sides (often called side A and side B). **Analog signals** are very small: the sound needs to be amplified so you can then hear it through your speakers or headphones. DJs often use 12-inch vinyls which have extra-long mixes or music specially made for DJs to play and mix. They come in either 33 rpm or 45 rpm.

Vinyl deck features

1. POWER SWITCH turns the deck on or off

2. PLATTER/PLATE is the spinning part you put the record onto

3. PLATTER/SLIP MAT sits on top of the platter and protects the record from being damaged

4. COUNTERWEIGHT helps to balance the tone arm and keep it from skipping across the record or damaging the needle

11. EARTH WIRE connects to the mixer's earth connections and protects you if there is a fault in the electrical system

10. SPINDLE sticks up from the center for the vinyl record to fit over

9. START/STOP BUTTON starts or stops playing the record

5. TONE ARM gets gently lifted and placed onto the record

6. PITCH CONTROL alters the speed or sound of the record so that you can get two records to play together at the same speed

8. HEADSHELL picks up the music signal on the record so that you can hear the sound (it is very delicate so be careful not to damage it!)

7. RPM BUTTON controls the revolutions per minute (RPM) to either 33 rpm or 45 rpm

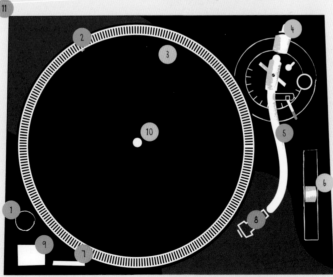

THE DJ MIXER

A mixer does exactly what it says—it mixes the music together from the CD or vinyl decks! The mixer sits between the two vinyl or CD decks. There are many different types of DJ mixers, but they all have the same main features. When you are starting out, you will only need a small 2-channel mixer.

YOU CAN USE THE CROSS FADER TO MIX THE MUSIC, BUT IT IS MAINLY USED FOR MIXING HIP-HOP MUSIC AND **SCRATCHING.**

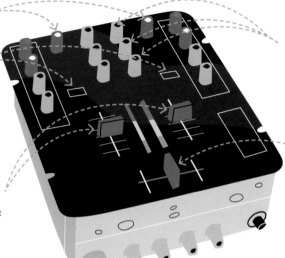

GAIN BUTTONS alter the volume levels of each individual input channel

CUE BUTTONS help the DJ choose and listen to the music in the headphones, before and during the mix

VOLUME FADERS are sliders that mix the music from the two decks in and out

EQ BUTTONS alter the hi-, mid-, and low-sound frequencies in the music

CROSS FADER crosses over from the left deck to right and vice versa

HEADPHONES AND SPEAKERS

Headphones let the DJ listen to the music to choose the next song and cue it, so it is ready to play. Speakers allow you and others to hear the music you are DJing. The better the speaker, the better the music will sound—within reason! Active speakers have amplifiers built into them, so you can connect them directly to the mixer's outputs. Passive speakers need a separate amplifier connected to them in order for you to hear any sound.

DIGITAL SOFTWARE

Using digital software is one of the easiest ways to begin DJing, and there are a lot of different programs you can use. All you need is a computer, a DJ program, and—if possible—a controller to help better control the software.

Software is often free to download or comes on a CD. DJ software contains two digital decks where you drag and drop music to mix. Some programs have a digital mixer but it's better to have a controller to control the software and mix. All software has the same basic features as vinyl or CD decks.

DJ DIGITAL SOFTWARE

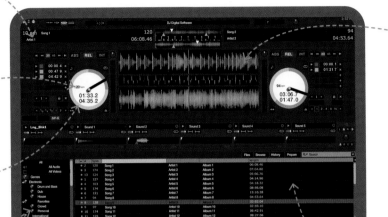

SONG NAME displays the name/title of the song playing

DECK 1 AND 2 virtual digital decks

TRACK TIME shows the total track time and/or track time remaining

AUDIO FOLDERS section for main music folders

WAVEFORM DISPLAYS show the visual track position playing in waveform format

INDIVIDUAL TRACK SONGS/POOL displays the individual track for you to drag and drop onto the digital decks

EXAMPLE OF A DJ CONTROLLER

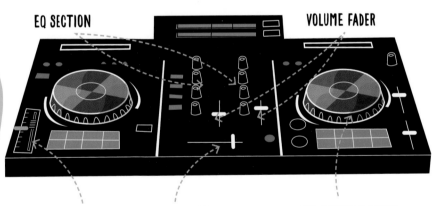

EQ SECTION

VOLUME FADER

PITCH CONTROL

CROSS FADER

JOG CONTROL WHEEL

HANDY TIP!
You can search online to find various DJ software programs. They often come with a free trial period, and if you like it you can then buy the full version.

DJ CONTROLLER

A controller is a physical unit that controls the software. It has two mini DJ decks, or jog wheels, and a mixer. It connects to your PC or laptop using a USB cable.

DJ APPS

You can also get DJ apps on your phone. DJay Pro, for example, has everything you need to spin tunes, and it's really cheap too!

SOUND CARDS

A sound card changes digital music files into audio signals. Without one, you can't hear the music! Your laptop will have one built in but it may not be very good, so buying an external sound card is a good idea. Some DJ controllers also have sound cards built in, but some don't, so you might need to get one depending on which controller you choose.

CHOOSING A SETUP

It's best to try out different options before buying equipment to make sure you don't waste your money! The easiest option is probably to go the software route, then buy and add hardware later once you have mastered the basics.

Tip 1: CHECK YOUR EQUIPMENT

Let's make sure you have everything you need. Look back at the lists on page 5 to check your equipment. Remember, the kit you need will be different depending on whether you are going the hardware or the software route.

Tip 2: ASK FOR ADVICE

Before buying any equipment in a shop, ask to try it out first. Always seek advice beforehand about what may be the best equipment for you. You can do research on the internet or talk to other DJs.

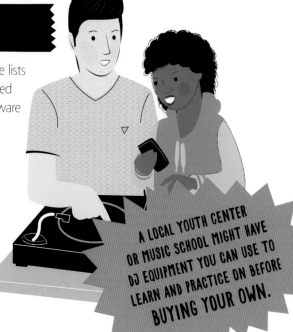

A LOCAL YOUTH CENTER OR MUSIC SCHOOL MIGHT HAVE DJ EQUIPMENT YOU CAN USE TO LEARN AND PRACTICE ON BEFORE **BUYING YOUR OWN.**

Tip 3: STAY SAFE!

DJing involves using electricity, so you must always be careful. Here are some ways that you can stay safe while DJing.

- DO read all hardware manuals thoroughly before setting up any equipment.
- DON'T switch on the main electric power until you have finished connecting all the equipment.

- DO use a flat, strong surface to put your equipment on. Unstable surfaces can cause equipment to fall on you.
- DON'T leave any cables lying around, as they could cause you to trip and fall.
- DON'T play music loudly for long periods of time, especially when using headphones. High volume can seriously damage your ears.

Tip 4: PROTECT YOUR EQUIPMENT

Make sure that all master volume buttons and faders are turned down or off before switching the power on or off for any hardware. If you leave them up, it can blow and permanently damage your speakers.

TO PROTECT YOUR EARS AND YOUR EQUIPMENT, REMEMBER THE CORRECT ORDER IN WHICH TO TURN THINGS ON AND OFF!

Hardware setup: vinyl/CD

LEFT CD OR VINYL TURNTABLE

RIGHT SPEAKER

MIXER

LEFT SPEAKER

HEADPHONES

RIGHT CD OR VINYL TURNTABLE

HANDY TIP!

If you're using vinyl decks, then you need to connect them to the PHONO inputs. If you are using CD decks, then you need to connect them to the CD/LINE inputs.

1. Connect the turntables, as shown, to the mixer channel inputs.

2. Connect the MAIN Left (L) and Right (R) outputs on the back of the mixer to the inputs of each speaker.

3. Connect the headphones to the mixer.

4. Turn on the power to the mixer first, then turn on the power to the speakers.

5. When you have finished, switch off the speakers first, and the mixer decks second.

Software setup

LEFT SPEAKER

DJ CONTROLLER

RIGHT SPEAKER

LAPTOP

HEADPHONES

1. Connect the controller to your laptop using a USB cable.

2. Connect the controller's main volume outputs to the speakers. If your controller doesn't have these outputs, then connect a soundcard to the laptop and connect its volume outputs to the speakers.

3. Connect the headphones to the controller.

4. Switch on the power to the controller first and then the speakers second.

5. When you have finished, turn off the speakers first, then the controller, and then the laptop.

FEELING THE BEAT!

Now that you have a basic overview of the equipment, the next step is learning about the beat, or the rhythm. The beat is one of the main things DJs use when mixing music together, especially dance music. Counting the beat is not hard and once you learn the basics, it will really help you with your mixing skills. It just takes a bit of learning and practice!

INTRODUCTION TO MUSIC THEORY

In the DJ world, music is made up of **rhythms**, **sounds**, **beats**, and **phrases**. To be able to DJ, you actually don't need to know much about music theory. Knowing some of the theory will be helpful, but DJs tend to just listen to the music and "feel" its emotions, rhythms, flow, and beats.

ONE REASON THAT DJING IS SO POPULAR IS THAT ANYBODY—NO MATTER WHAT THEIR BACKGROUND OR EDUCATION—CAN GIVE IT A TRY AND LEARN TO DO IT!

Know the lingo

Here are some basic terms that every DJ should know!

- **RHYTHM:** the flow of the music, which dances around and between the beats

- **BEATS:** the main pulse or heartbeat, providing a solid foundation to the track

- **PHRASES:** sections or parts of a song that fit together like a jigsaw puzzle, telling you where you are in the song

- **BARS:** the segments that the beats fit into, which repeat throughout the whole track

WHY ARE BEATS IMPORTANT?

Beats help the DJ to be able to mix from one song into the next song smoothly and without any gaps. The beat also helps the producer or artist to make the song in the first place. And it helps the audience to feel the music and dance to it!

WHAT IS THE BEAT?

The beat is basically the main drum beat that makes you dance! For example, house music uses a steady 4/4 beat or drum pattern throughout. This pattern helps the DJ to mix the record or track smoothly from one track to the next.

A song can be described as either **upbeat**, meaning it's full of energy and very active, or **downbeat**, which is slower, chilled, and more relaxed.

The beat can be "on beat" which means it would be directly on the 1-2-3-4. Dance music is typically on beat. It can also be "off beat" which means it would swing more between the main beat like 1, and a 2, and a 3, and a 4. Jazz music uses a lot of off beats!

USING THE BEAT

Counting the beat helps a DJ mix in the next record. Most songs have the same beat structure, which makes them easier to follow and mix with. Different music styles, such as dance, hip-hop, and swing, each have their own beat styles.

HANDY TIP!

Think of a beat as a pulse, or a heartbeat. You know that your heart beats at a regular rhythm: this is the same principle as the beat in dance music.

SUPERSTAR TIP

LISTEN TO SOME OF YOUR FAVORITE SONGS AND PAY ATTENTION TO HOW THEY USE THE BEAT.

COUNTING BEATS

In most songs the beat goes from 1 to 4 and then repeats. You can also count from 1 to 8 and then repeat, if that's easier for you. A song's beat is normally a constant rhythm, because a steady beat is easier to dance to!

Tip 1: COUNT ALONG

Before you start mixing, you need to know how to find the first beat in a song. The best way to begin is to find a dance song or track that has a beat starting from the very beginning of the song. Then all you need to do is start counting from 1 to 4 as soon as the beat starts and keep repeating it.

As you get more practice, you will start to see that many musical elements start or "come in" on the first beat. For example, a singer will start singing on number 1 of the beat. Of course, the singer may start later on in the song, but it will still be on the first beat of that part in the song!

Tip 2: WRITE IT DOWN

Music can be written down in a form called musical notation. People who play musical instruments such as the violin use notation so that they know which notes to play and what the rhythm is. The example below shows how a 4/4 beat would be written down. Notice how steady and constant the beat is: it has the same space in between each of the beats.

HANDY TIP!
Practice by clapping your hands and counting to 4 or to 8, and then repeat it over and over again!

Tip 3: CLAP IT OUT

Below shows an example of hand claps on the beat. Try it yourself and copy the pattern shown. How many complete hand clap beats are there?

SEARCH ONLINE FOR VIDEOS THAT DEMONSTRATE COUNTING BEATS. THERE ARE A LOT OF TUTORIALS ONLINE TO HELP YOU.

Tip 4: FIND THE BEAT

Practice finding the first beat on a vinyl record. First, find a dance track that has a beat that starts from the very beginning. **Cue the record**, which means putting the needle onto the record at the beginning. Gently allow the record to spin through your fingers until you hear the very first beat. Stop or hold the record gently as soon as you hear it. Now gently bring the record backward until you go just past the first beat, and there you have it! If you gently move the record forward and backward over that beat, it should sound nice and clear!

WHAT IS A BAR?

Now that you know what a beat is, the next step is to understand what a bar is! A bar is simply a measure that we use to break up and count music. Each bar is a small amount of time. All the bars in a song will normally have the same number of beats. When bars are repeated, it is called a "loop."

Putting music into bars is basically just putting the individual beats into groups. For DJs, a bar is usually made up of either four or eight individual beats.

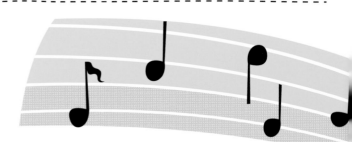

EXAMPLE 1

Here's an example for a song that has four beats in a bar. You would count it like this:

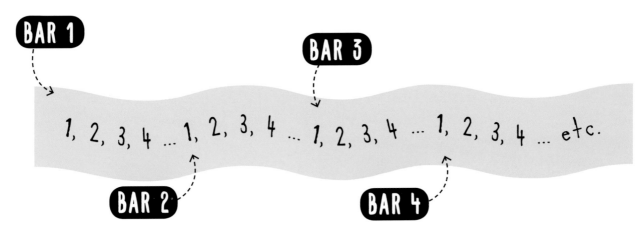

EXAMPLE 2

You can also count from 1 to 8. It is up to the individual whether they prefer to count in groups of 4 or 8. At the end of the day, it is the same thing. Here is an example of the same song with eight beats.

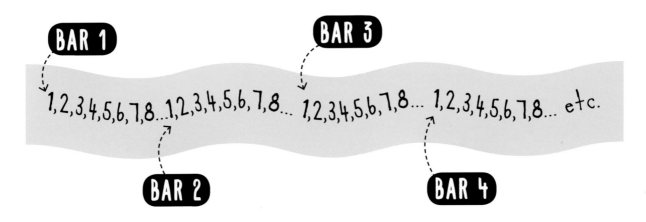

PUTTING THEORY INTO PRACTICE

Now, find a song that you really like, listen to it carefully, and see if you can figure out the beat. Can you figure out where the first beat in each bar starts? If you can, that's fantastic, and you're off to a great start. Every DJ needs to learn where the first beat of each bar is—this is how we mix! Note it and then ask your parent, friend, brother, or sister to try to find the first beat. Did they say the same as you? If not, then you can discuss why you think it's different.

SUPERSTAR TIP

REMEMBER: A BAR IS MADE UP OF BEATS, AND THE BEAT IS THE RHYTHM YOU FEEL AND DANCE TO! A DJ NEEDS TO KNOW HOW TO COUNT TO 4 AND REPEAT IT, AND TO LEARN WHERE THE FIRST BEAT IN EACH BAR IS.

MIXING IT UP

In this chapter you will learn about what mixing is, along with the basic skills you'll need to be able to mix tracks together. Once you learn how to use the mixer, you'll be able to start creating your own "mini DJ mix." Mixing is an essential part of DJing, each DJ will develop his or her own individual style of mixing. But to start, it's very important that you understand the basic skills. You'll need to practice!

WHAT IS MIXING?

Mixing is taking two or more pieces of music and mixing or blending them together, so that they become one combined mix. A mix can be just two songs or up to hundreds of songs—it all depends how long you want the mix to be! A mix can be recorded to create a CD, to be played on TV or on the radio, or it can be performed live in front of an audience.

In dance music, mixing is especially important. Dance DJs use the beat to be able to mix smoothly from one track or song into the next one. This is also known as beat matching or beat mixing.

WHY MIX?

When you mix, you are creating a story or a journey through the music. In fact, you are creating your own DJ style! DJs use mixing to create different moods and feelings. In the early days of DJing, mixing was created as a way of playing for much longer. This allowed DJs to be more inventive and creative. When you are doing your own mixing, remember that creativity is key!

GIVE IT A TRY!

Take a song, record, or CD that you like, experiment and play around with the different speeds, play with the pitch control, and play it backward. How does it all sound? How could you use this when you are creating a mix?

HANDY TIP!
Learn your music! The greater your knowledge of different music styles, the better you'll be at mixing.

What to mix

You can mix whatever you like! Try experimenting with different music. You could try playing music at different speeds and seeing how it sounds. Once you find a few styles that you like, you can start to focus on how best to mix those styles together.

Jazz music

Drum n Bass

Hip-hop music

Heavy metal music

Dance music

Pop music

Ambient music

MIXING TECHNIQUES

There are many different ways of mixing, but here are the basic elements that will help you get started. The more you learn, the better your mixing skills will become. You will develop your own style and learn to rock the party!

"BLENDING" MIX EXERCISE

Start by trying a very basic "blending" mix, to help you get used to using the decks and the mixer.

1 First, choose two songs. Put one on the left deck and the other song on the right. (Make sure both volume faders on the mixer are down.)

2 Start to play the first song on the left-hand deck. Fade up the first song using the left fader on the mixer. You should now hear the music playing!

3 Now start playing the second song on the right-hand deck. While the first song is still playing, mix in the second song using the right-hand fader on the mixer. Now you have the two songs playing out together!

4 Slowly fade down or out the first song using the left-hand side fader. That's all there is to it! You have blended your first DJ mix.

DON'T WORRY ABOUT HOW IT ALL SOUNDS, JUST HAVE FUN AND **EXPERIMENT!**

"MATCH UP BEATS" EXERCISE

It's time to give beat mixing a try. Beat mixing is when you match the beats on two different tracks and then mix the songs together.

1 Choose two dance tracks to mix. Start playing the first track on the left-hand deck, and turn up the left fader on the mixer so you can hear it playing.

2 Now put the other track on the right-hand deck and use your headphones to find the first beat.

3 Now you need to listen to the first track while you line up or "cue" the second track. The aim is to start the second track playing in time to the first track. If the two tracks sound like one track playing together, that means the beats are perfectly matched.

4 You can now mix in the second track on the right fader while the first one is still playing, then slowly mix out the first track on the left fader. It may not be perfect, but the more you practice, the easier it will become.

> WHAT IS TEMPO? TEMPO MEANS THE SPEED AT WHICH THE TRACK OR SONG PLAYS, OR THE SPEED OF THE BEAT WITHIN IT.

HANDY TIP!

It is much easier to learn by playing the same track on both decks. If you can't get two identical copies of a track, try to find two that are very similar in tempo with a strong beat and few other musical elements.

FIX ANY PROBLEMS

When both tracks are playing together, listen carefully. How do they sound together? If the music sounds all messy and jumbled up, that means the beats are not matching up together. If this happens, be patient, start the second track from the beginning, and try again! If you are playing two different tracks with slightly different speeds, then you will need to adjust the pitch control on the second deck to get the speed playing in time. Practice makes perfect!

CUTTING IN THE MIX

Cutting (or "dropping") means that instead of fading a mix in or out, you add in the mix quickly. This technique is often used in hip-hop music, where the beats are quite different and harder to mix together.

"CUTTING IN THE MIX" EXERCISE

Try using the cross fader on the mixer to do a drop-in mix.

1 Choose two tracks. Put the first one on the left-hand deck and put the cross fader fully over to the left-hand side.

2 Fade up both the volume faders on the mixer and start to play the first track.

3 Put the second track on the right-hand deck and use the headphones to cue it up to the beginning.

4 Find the first beat on the second track and quickly move the cross fader fully across to the right-hand side. At the same time, press play on the second deck to start playing the second track. You have "dropped" it into the mix!

HANDY TIP!
Drop in the second track sharply as the first track comes to the end of the 8 count phrase. You need to be quick!

GOOD MIX, BAD MIX

So what makes a good mix and what makes a not-so-good mix? A good mix will sound nice and smooth, with no big gaps between songs or sudden jumps in volume. When people listen or dance to a good mix they sometimes won't even notice the mix blend between the two tracks! A bad mix will sound like it's muddled and jumbled up. It won't be smooth and the beats will clash and sound messy.

SUPERSTAR TIP

IF YOU ARE USING CD DECKS OR DIGITAL SOFTWARE, THE DROP-IN WILL BE IMMEDIATE WHEN YOU PRESS THE STOP AND START BUTTONS TOGETHER. IF YOU ARE USING VINYL, THERE WILL BE A SLIGHT DELAY AS THE SECOND RECORD STARTS PLAYING.

Tips for getting it right:

- Take the time to find the beat—don't rush!
- Try lots of different things until you find something that works.
- Don't be scared of trying something new or different!
- Search online for tutorials on how to mix.
- Make the time to practice.
- Learn how to use the functions on your equipment. If you don't know your equipment, it will be harder to get a good mix!
- If it goes wrong, just take a deep breath, smile, and start again.
- The most important thing is to have fun!

HOW DID YOU DO?

When you are doing a mix, think about how it went and what you could try differently next time. Did the songs match and fit together? Was the choice of song styles a good match? Did the beats match together, or did they clash or go out of time? If they were out of time, how could you correct this for your next mix?

LEARN YOUR MUSIC SO YOU WILL KNOW WHERE THE BEST BREAKS ARE TO DROP IN YOUR MIXES.

SCRATCHING

Scratching is one of the most famous DJ art forms. But what exactly is it? In this chapter you will learn about the history of scratching, as well as picking up some of the basic scratch techniques. As with all DJ skills, you need to start with the basics and then practice, listen to what you are doing, and get into the groove!

WHAT IS SCRATCHING?

Scratching means taking one noise or sound and moving it backward and forward repeatedly while another piece of music is playing. This means you **scratch** to the music. Scratching originated as part of the hip-hop movement, where vinyl DJs began to experiment with different ways to mix or drop in the next beat. They began to create noises and sound effects with the records, using them not only to mix songs, but to cut and drop into the next tune too.

DJs WHO SCRATCH

Scratching is mainly used by hip-hop DJs. They scratch over the beats of the other records that are playing, and they use scratching as part of the mixing of songs and beats. Other DJ styles can also use scratching, so there are no limits to what you can scratch to.

BEAT JUGGLING

A new technique called "beat juggling" soon developed out of scratching. **Beat juggling** is exactly what it sounds like—a DJ gets two beats and switches in and out and between them. This creates new rhythms, using scratching as a basis. As DJs developed the technique, scratching became an art form all of its own. It is often referred to as "turntablism" skills. It is very closely linked to hip-hop music and also with breakdancing.

GO TO SEE A DJ BATTLE IF YOU CAN. YOU'LL BE ABLE TO PICK UP ON NEW IDEAS AND TRICKS, AND EXPERIENCE THE VIBE OF A BATTLE!

DJ BATTLES

Each year international competitions called "battles" are held, where top scratch DJs compete with one another to see who has the best skills! Scratch DJs are also a big part of breaking competitions. **Breaking** is a dance form where dancers do amazing moves and skills on the floor, challenging one another as individuals or as part of a team. Scratch DJs always play at such events.

SUCCESSFUL SCRATCHING

Scratching is all about creating sounds and patterns and rhythms, so it's very important to listen to what you are scratching while you are doing it. How does it sound? Is it in time to any other music that you are playing? Does it sound good?

DOS AND DON'TS

Top DJs make scratching look easy, but it takes practice to learn how to do it right. Here are some tips to help as you learn:

- DO be careful when using vinyl for scratching.
- DON'T use your grandparents' old records or record player. They are not designed for scratching and will probably break!

- DO watch online tutorials to help you understand and master scratching skills.
- DON'T give up. Learning to scratch takes time, determination, and patience!
- DO have fun, experiment, and try out new ideas.
- DO watch other scratch DJs for tips and advice!

SCRATCHING VINYL

Scratch DJs have special records and CDs which are specifically made for scratching. They call them "battle tools!" These tools contain loads of different sounds, noises, and beats, and some of them have become very well known. If you listen to a lot of hip-hop music, you may recognize some of the most famous sounds.

Tip 1: SET UP YOUR TURNTABLES

If you are using vinyl, arrange your turntables as shown below. This will give you more space to use your hands. When you are scratching, you will move the record and the record arm a lot more than when you are mixing normally, so you need more space!

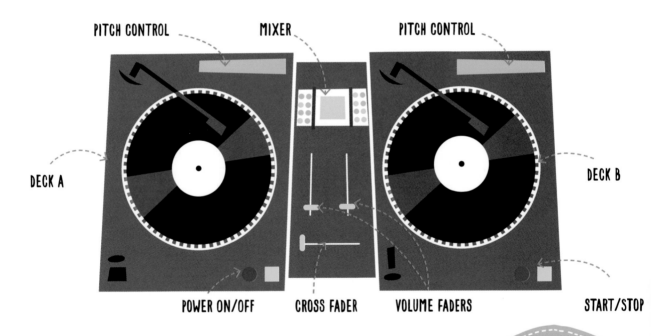

PITCH CONTROL   MIXER   PITCH CONTROL

DECK A   DECK B

POWER ON/OFF   CROSS FADER   VOLUME FADERS   START/STOP

Tip 2: LEARN TO USE YOUR MIXER

Part of learning to scratch involves developing some specific skills using the DJ mixer. The most important thing is learning how to use the faders and the cross fader properly.

HANDY TIP!
If you're having trouble getting it right, take a deep breath, relax, and then start again from the beginning.

Tip 3: ASSEMBLE YOUR SOUNDS

Get yourself some scratch sounds on CD or vinyl, or download them. You'll also need to get some **instrumentals** to scratch to. These are basic hip-hop drum beats, without any other music. They are great for scratching to and for learning how to beat juggle. You can get them on vinyl, CD, or online.

Tip 4: WATCH AND LEARN

There are plenty of online scratching tutorials. Do a search for video tutorials that can teach you how to scratch and to learn some new techniques.

ALWAYS GET YOUR **PARENTS' PERMISSION** BEFORE RESEARCHING ONLINE!

SCRATCH 1: THE "BABY SCRATCH"

The baby scratch is the simplest scratch to learn. To do it, you need to keep the cross fader open in the middle position on the mixer.

1 If you are using vinyl, put the scratch record onto either deck. (If using a CD or software, put the CD or digital sound onto one of the decks.)

2 Holding the record still with one hand, place the needle carefully onto it and find a sound that you like. (If you are using a CD or software, find a sound and hold the jog wheel in place.)

3 Move the record or jog wheel forward and backward over the sound. Start off slowly, then gradually speed up as you get used to it.

4 Now play some music or an instrumental beat on the other record deck and practice doing the baby scratch to the beat.

USING A BABY SCRATCH

You could use this scratch technique to start off the song, or you could use it while another song is playing. It can add a bit of variety, sound, or extra skills to your DJ performance. It works especially well with hip-hop music, but it can also be used for other types of music. Experiment and see where you can use it!

SCRATCH 2: THE "FORWARD SCRATCH"

The forward scratch is also called "cutting." It is the same as the baby scratch, but uses the cross fader.

1 Put the scratch record on the left-hand deck.

2 Find your sound with the cross fader open (in the middle position).

3 Move the record forward and play the sound, then stop the record or jog wheel.

4 When you bring the record backward to find the beginning of the sound again, close the cross fader to the right-hand side of the mixer at the same time. This will cut out the sound as you bring the record backward.

5 When you play the record again, open the cross fader to the middle position, and keep repeating. You are now are using both hands at the same time!

Once you get the hang of this, you can play some music or an instrumental beat on the other deck and do the scratch to the beat.

IT IS CALLED **CUTTING** BECAUSE IT'S LIKE CUTTING OUT OR CHOPPING UP PARTS OF A SOUND. YOU ONLY HEAR THE PARTS THAT YOU WANT AND CUT OUT THE REST!

USING THE FORWARD SCRATCH

You could use this scratch if you have a vocal "a capella" to add over the top of another song. The forward scratch cuts out the noise while you reverse back to the beginning of the a cappella vocal.

WHAT IS AN A CAPPELLA?

An **a cappella** is a vocal without any music behind it. As the music is removed, you can use it over the top of another instrumental song. (An **instrumental** is a song with no words.) This is sometimes referred to as creating a live new remix.

HANDY TIP!
Once you can do the forward scratch, try reversing it and doing a reverse scratch. It may take some practice but you'll learn a whole new scratch!

SCRATCH 3: THE "SCRIBBLE SCRATCH"

The scribble (or "wobble scratch," as it is sometimes called) involves finding a sound on the record and literally making it wobble!

1 Put your scratch record on one of the decks. Find a good sound to use, with the cross fader open.

2 Hold the vinyl or CD still over the top of the sound.

3 Gently start to wobble the record in small shaky movements, producing a scribble (or a wobble) sound!

USING THE SCRIBBLE SCRATCH

You will need to keep your arm tense to get this action to sound right, and to stop the needle from jumping on the record! Once you get the hang of it, you can try this scratch at different speeds. Start off slowly, then speed up or slow down. Have fun with it, and see how creative you can make it sound!

SUPERSTAR TIP

IF YOU WANT TO BECOME A HIP-HOP DJ, YOU WILL DEFINITELY NEED TO LEARN AND MASTER THE SKILL OF SCRATCHING. A BIG PART OF SCRATCHING IS BEING ABLE TO USE THE DJ MIXER IN DIFFERENT WAYS, ESPECIALLY THE CROSS FADER. SEE IF YOU CAN CREATE YOUR OWN NEW SCRATCHES!

PRACTICE MAKES PERFECT

Now you need to practice putting your DJ skills together. This will help you develop your skills, and your musical awareness and confidence, too! Here are a few exercises to help you practice. The more you practice, the easier it will all become!

HANDY TIP!
Don't be too fast with the faders! Instead, aim for a smooth mix. Using both hands will give you more control.

TUTORIAL 1: "BLEND MIXING"

Smoothly fading in one song to the next takes a lot of practice. You need to be nice and smooth with the volume faders on the mixer, so that it sounds great!

1 Choose two tracks, listen to them, and make a note of where you think would be good points to start mixing the next song in or out.

2 Start playing the first track, and fade up the left volume fader so that the music is playing out of the speakers.

3 Using the headphones, prepare the second track, to make sure it is ready when you get to the mixing place on the first track. It's a good idea to start playing the second track from the beginning (rather than the middle), then practice blending it into the mix while the first track is still playing.

4 Now practice mixing in the second track at different points later in the song.

5 For more practice, reverse it and blend the first track into the second track. You are now extending the mix and making it last longer. This will be useful for the next skill!

TUTORIAL 2: "BEAT MATCHING"

The key to good beat matching is learning to control the speed of the tracks so that they match exactly together and stay in time. You do this by using the pitch control, which allows the track to be played a bit faster or slower. Moving the pitch control backward will slow it down, moving it forward will speed it up.

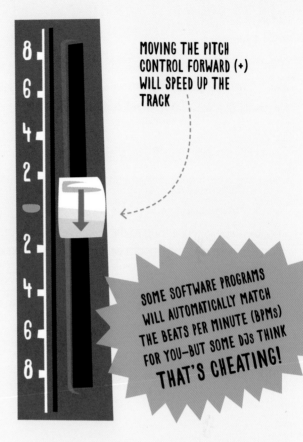

MOVING THE PITCH CONTROL FORWARD (+) WILL SPEED UP THE TRACK

SOME SOFTWARE PROGRAMS WILL AUTOMATICALLY MATCH THE BEATS PER MINUTE (BPMs) FOR YOU—BUT SOME DJs THINK **THAT'S CHEATING!**

1 Start by choosing two tracks that have strong clear beats from the beginning, and are the same speed—or as close as possible!

2 With both the mixer volume faders up, start playing the first track.

3 Find the first beat at the beginning of the second track. You can remind yourself how to do this on page 19.

4 Counting the beats on the first track, gently drop in the first beat of the second track. If you push it off too hard it will rush ahead of the first track, but if you let go too softly it will lag behind!

5 How does the speed compare to the first track? If you think it's too fast or slow, adjust the pitch control. If you are using vinyl decks you'll have to go by "feel" to know how much to adjust it. If you are using digital or CD decks, you can use the visual tempo indicators on the screen. They give the speeds in beats per minute (bpm).

6 Once you've adjusted the pitch control, take the second track back to the beginning and try again, until you have both tracks playing together and at the same speed.

WAVEFORMS

If you are using a digital setup, you will see the individual tracks playing as waveforms on the screen. The different colors in a waveform represent different instruments. You can see the beats in a waveform, which looks like this:

THE BEAT IS: 1 AND 2 AND 3 AND 4 AND...

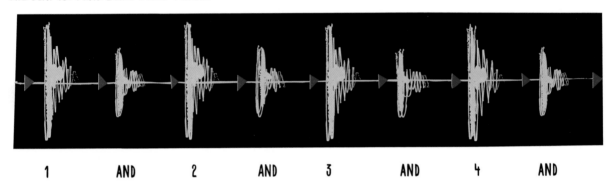

| 1 | AND | 2 | AND | 3 | AND | 4 | AND |

USING WAVEFORMS TO BEAT MATCH

You can "see" the beat in a waveform, so you can use it to help you beat match! Below are waveforms from two tracks. You can see that they are not playing in time and when mixed together they will sound messy and jumbled up.

This obviously needs to be fixed! Firstly you need to drop in the first beat of the second track in time, otherwise you'll never know if both beats are actually playing at the same speed. If you mistime the first beat drop, the tracks will always be out of sync. If the track is still playing out of sync after dropping the first beat in correctly, you could alter the pitch of one track (the one that you are preparing to be mixed) to make it faster or slower.

TWO WAVEFORMS THAT
ARE NOT ALIGNED

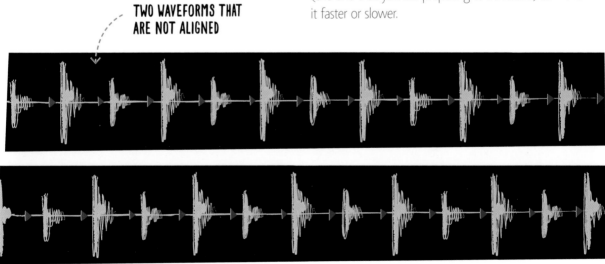

GETTING IT RIGHT

Here are two waveforms playing in time together. The beats of the two tracks are in time with each other, the bpm of both tracks are the same, and the first beats are matched together. This will give you a good mix!

TWO WAVEFORMS THAT ARE ALIGNED

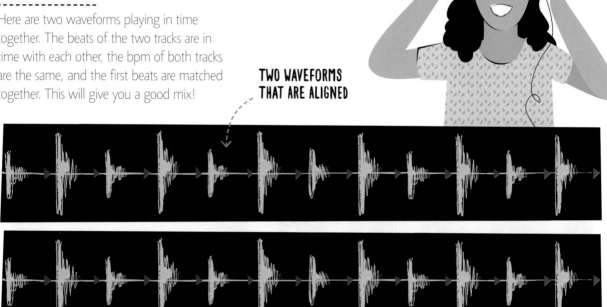

TUTORIAL 3: COMBINING MIXING AND SCRATCHING

This is a great skill to practice! You just need to choose two tracks and decide whether you want to blend mix or beat match them.

1 Prepare and play the first track.

2 Place the scratch vinyl (or CD or digital file) onto the other deck. Using your headphones, select the scratch sounds that you want to use.

3 Practice scratching to the first track. Think about what kind of sounds would work best, and where in the song scratching would sound best. If the track already has a lot of music, sounds, and singing, then scratching on top of that will probably be too much. Use your judgment (and your ears!) to make the scratching fit with the music.

4 Now it's time to prepare your second track, ready to mix in. If you are doing a beat mix, you will need to allow more time to prepare the beats so that they are in time. Keep your eye on how much time you have left before the first song finishes! When you are ready, move the cross fader to the middle position and fade up the volume fader to mix in the second track.

5 Once you have done the mix, try scratching to the second track. This time, the scratch record will be using the other deck (where the first track was before). Some DJs use a setup with three decks (for example, two record decks and a CD deck) so they can dedicate one deck just for scratching!

PREPARING A DJ SET

Once you're confident in your mixing and scratching skills, it's time to prepare your first DJ set. There are a lot of things to think about in order to produce a good set. Who is the audience and what's the occasion? These will affect your choices about what to play.

WHAT IS A DJ SET?

A DJ set is where a DJ plays and mixes together a lot of tracks over a period of time. It might be played to a live audience at a concert or party, or played on the radio. A set could even be designed for making a demo CD! To prepare a set, the DJ needs to choose the music and the order in which to play it. Choosing the right opening and closing tracks can make all the difference!

Tip 1: PLAN IT OUT

A great DJ set may sound effortless, but it's all carefully planned. Think about who will be listening to your set: what kind of crowd will it be? What mood will they be in? What about the music? Does it have to be a particular style, or could you use a mixture of different styles? How long will the set last? This will help you figure out how much music you need. Finally, make sure you know what equipment you will be using.

Tip 2: CHOOSE A KILLER OPENING

The way you start off your DJ set can create a big impact! It could be a famous speech, a sound clip from your favorite movie, or a piece of music that you love. The more distinctive it is, the more you will stand out! You could also just start off by playing the first song really slowly, then speeding it up to its normal speed...or use a big blast of sound to announce your arrival!

IF YOU FIND A GREAT INTRO AND USE IT FOR EVERY SET, IT COULD BECOME YOUR **TRADEMARK!**

Tip 3: USE LINKS

You don't have to just mix from one song to the next all the time! A **link** is a sample soundbite (such as a voice sample, short speech, or scratch sample) that you can use to link the tracks. Links can add a more personal touch to your mix and make it more interesting. Think about a radio broadcast, where you often hear short ads and voice-overs between the music. These soundbites help make the show longer and more interesting and they can do the same for your DJ set!

You could use scratch sounds as links, or find a speech or sound clips from a film, then use them as part of the mixing to link one song to the next. You could also play or mix in the links over the top as a track is playing. You'll definitely need to plan and practice this, to keep your set as smooth as possible.

CREATING A MOOD

When preparing your mix, think about what it will be used for. Will it be a recording for your own personal use, or for your friends to listen to? When you prepare a set for recording you have to think about how someone will feel when they listen to it. What kind of vibe do you want to create? The songs you choose will help you create the mood in your DJ set.

MOOD

When you play live you still want to create a mood, but you will also need to be able to react to the audience. You should prepare your set carefully, but have some flexibility so that you can respond to the crowd's reaction as you are playing. You may find that your audience isn't into the set you've prepared! So it pays to have extra music that you can add into your set if needed.

CUE POINTS

A cue is a specific point in a song that you want to mark, so that you can use it as a starting point in your mix or to find a particular scratch sound. Remember, you don't always have to start from the beginning of a song. By setting a cue to start later on in a song, you can mix it in at a specific point that you really like!

HANDY TIP!
Know your records, so you know where the drops are, how the songs end and begin, and where the best parts are. The better you know your music, the better your set will be!

CUE POINTS ON DIGITAL DECKS

If you are using CD decks or software, it's easier to set up and store specific cue points. Every machine is different, so you will need to search online or read the manual for tips on how to set up cue points.

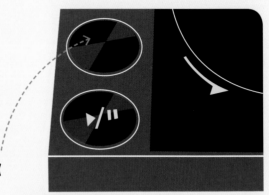

CUE BUTTON ON A CD DECK

CUE POINTS ON VINYL

You can also put cue points on a vinyl record in the form of sticker markers. You often see this on scratch records where the DJ likes to use particular sounds or beats.

**CUE POINTS (STICKERS)
MARKED ON A VINYL RECORD**

USING CUE POINTS

Setting up **cue points** in advance will help your DJ set go more smoothly. They let you easily find mixing points, do drop-in quick mixes, and find and store your favorite parts of a song. If you search online you'll find video tutorials on how to best use and set up cue points. Also check out the useful links on page 62. Take the time to learn how to use the cue points on your own equipment—you won't regret it!

WHERE TO SET CUE POINTS:

- At the beginning of a drum beat (on the first beat)
- At the beginning of a vocal section (on the first beat)
- At the beginning of a break section in the song
- At the beginning of a particular scratch sound

TUTORIAL 1: PRACTICE USING CUE POINTS

Once you've learned how to set cue points on your equipment, it's time to practice using them.

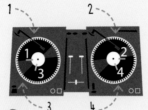

1 Select two tracks and find two points in each that you think would be good cue points to use for mixing. Choose a selection of music points, vocal points, and beat points as your cues.

2 Set up the cue points by using the cue button on your CD decks or by taping your vinyl decks. Make a list of your cue points, numbering them from 1 to 4.

3 Start off with the first cue point on your first song. This will be your introduction cue point.

4 Cue up your second track on the other deck, at the second cue point.

5 When you are ready, start the second track at the second cue point and bring it into the mix.

6 Go back to the first track and find the third cue point. When you are ready, bring it into the mix.

7 Go back to your second track and locate the fourth cue point. Set it up as before and mix it.

HOW DID IT GO?

If your mix didn't work well, think about how to fix it. Maybe you could have chosen better cue points, or set them up more carefully, or mixed them in a different order. There are always ways to make it better—that's part of becoming a DJ! Once you've gotten the hang of it, practice adding more cue points or using them in different ways.

SUPERSTAR TIP

THINK CAREFULLY ABOUT HOW YOU MAY WANT TO USE YOUR CUE POINTS SO THAT YOU GET THE BEST OUT OF THEM, AND REMEMBER TO BE PRECISE WHEN YOU MARK AND SET THEM UP!

TUTORIAL 2: CREATE A MINI DJ SET

It's time to put everything together and create your first mini DJ set! Once you've prepared and practiced this 15-minute set, you should be able to play it from the beginning to the end, with no stops or gaps.

1 Figure out how much music you will need to play for 15 minutes. For example, if you play each track for three minutes, you will need five tracks. (Of course, you might play some tracks for longer or shorter, so plan carefully.)

2 Put your chosen tracks into an order and find the best places to mix them. Set up any cue points that you would like to use. Decide whether you will use links or add any scratching.

3 Think about how you can best mix the tracks together. Will you be beat matching? If so, it's a good idea to order your tracks by speed, from the slowest to the fastest. (You can also pre-set the bpm to make your mixing smoother.)

4 Make sure that the equipment is all set up correctly and ready to go.

5 Take a deep breath, put on the first track, press play, and start your mix! If you go wrong or make a mistake, you can always stop and start again. Practice it a few times, and remember that you can change the order of tracks to find what works best.

HANDY TIP!
Once you're confident, play your mini set for your friends or family. This will start to get you used to playing in front of people.

RECORDING YOUR SET

Once you can play a DJ set, it's time to record it! You'll need to know how to use your equipment to get the best recording—and a few post-production tips will help ensure it sounds as good as possible.

WHY RECORD?

Recording a DJ mix means that you can listen back to it to hear what you sound like! It helps you see what does and doesn't work, so you can make improvements. Another good reason to record is that you can share your sets with friends. You could even send a copy to a promoter, who might like it and book you to do a gig!

REMEMBER TO **DOUBLE CHECK** THAT YOU HAVE PRESSED THE RECORD BUTTON BEFORE YOU START RECORDING!

Tip 1: STEREO OR MONO?

Most recording setups have two options: stereo or mono. Always choose stereo, as it will give you better sound. It means that your mix will play in both speakers (or headphones) and give you a nice, wide sound. If you record in mono, you will hear the music in both speakers, but you won't hear as much detail as you can in stereo mode.

MONO

STEREO

TOO FAR LEFT

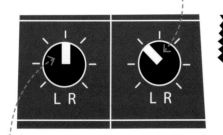

CENTER POSITION

Tip 2: GET THE BALANCE RIGHT

Make sure that your balance (also called **PAN**) level is in the center. If it is too far to the left-hand or right-hand side, your recorded mix will play more out of one side of the speakers than the other side. If it's balanced in the center, you will get a nice stereo mix!

WHAT YOU WILL NEED

In order to record your set, you will need some form of recording device or software program. The simplest option is when your DJ software does it for you! Some DJ programs allow you to record yourself while you are performing your DJ mix. You just have to hit the "record" function before starting to play your set.

You will need to see if the software you have chosen to use has this feature built in. Check your manual, or search online to find out. Two good programs with this function are Serato DJ and Virtual DJ Free.

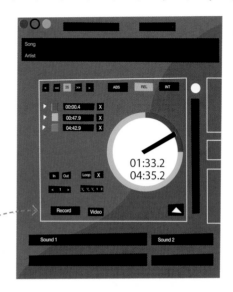

RECORD FUNCTION

USING SEPARATE SOFTWARE

If your DJ software doesn't have an internal recording function (or if you are using CD decks or vinyl decks), you will need a separate recording program. Audacity is a free piece of downloadable software that is good for beginners and gives you basic recording facilities.

Sound Forge is a more professional recording and editing software. It has good editing tools and comes in various packages, for beginners to advanced users. It's not free, but you can download a free trial version to try it out first.

HANDY TIP!
There are many other recording programs available. Do some research and try before you buy!

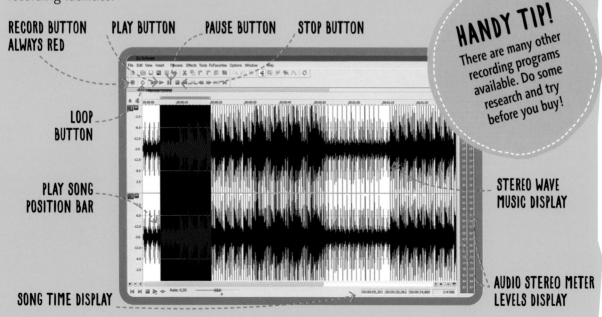

RECORD BUTTON ALWAYS RED

PLAY BUTTON

PAUSE BUTTON

STOP BUTTON

LOOP BUTTON

PLAY SONG POSITION BAR

STEREO WAVE MUSIC DISPLAY

SONG TIME DISPLAY

AUDIO STEREO METER LEVELS DISPLAY

RECORDING HARDWARE

Another option is to get some recording hardware, such as a CD recorder or a portable sound recording device like an MP3 recorder. A CD recorder will allow you to record your mix and burn it onto a CD right away, which is handy. If you use an MP3 recorder then you will need to transfer the recorded mix to your laptop so you can edit it or burn a CD.

POWER ON/OFF BUTTON

CD TRAY

VISUAL DISPLAY PANEL

RECORD BUTTON

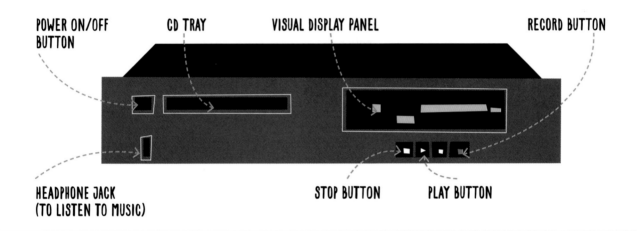

HEADPHONE JACK (TO LISTEN TO MUSIC)

STOP BUTTON

PLAY BUTTON

How to connect your recording device

To use recording hardware, you need to connect your recording output from the mixer into the record input on your hardware device. To connect a CD recording deck to a mixer, you will most likely need a stereo phono-to-phono lead. Connect one end into the left & right record IN on the CD recorder, and put the other end into the left & right record OUT on the mixer.

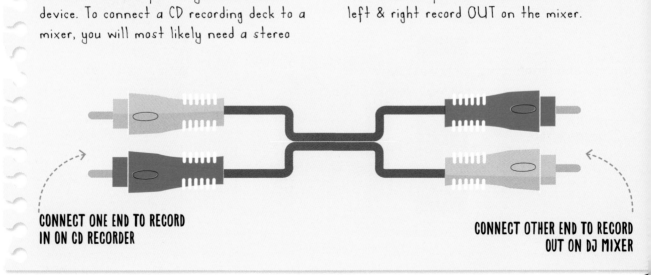

CONNECT ONE END TO RECORD IN ON CD RECORDER

CONNECT OTHER END TO RECORD OUT ON DJ MIXER

METER DISPLAY LEVELS

When you are recording your set, it's important that you set your recording levels correctly, so that you get a good recording of your mix. You don't want to record your mix too loudly. This will make your recording sound distorted and horrible, even if the mix itself was good. You can tell if you're recording too loudly because the level will be in the red. Be careful to keep your recording levels in the green, yellow, or amber areas. Remember that red means "danger," so stay out!

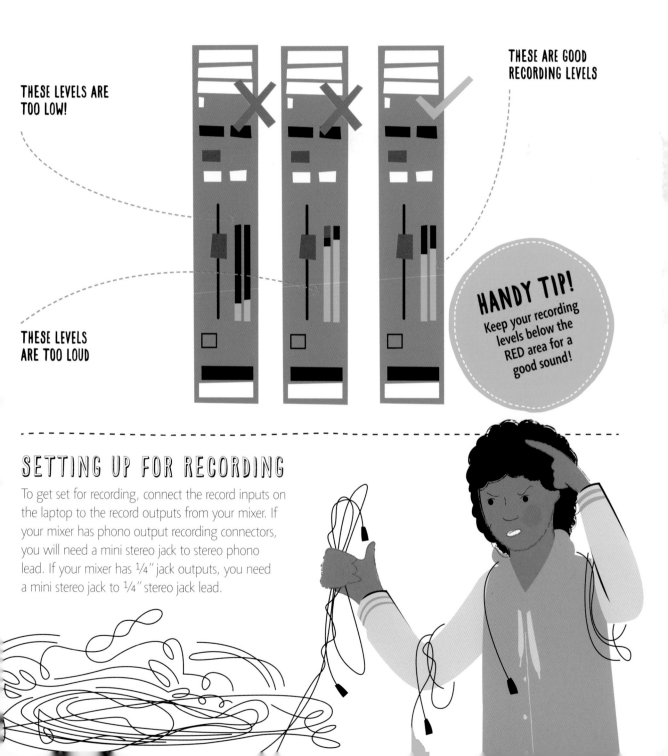

THESE ARE GOOD RECORDING LEVELS

THESE LEVELS ARE TOO LOW!

THESE LEVELS ARE TOO LOUD

HANDY TIP!
Keep your recording levels below the RED area for a good sound!

SETTING UP FOR RECORDING

To get set for recording, connect the record inputs on the laptop to the record outputs from your mixer. If your mixer has phono output recording connectors, you will need a mini stereo jack to stereo phono lead. If your mixer has ¼" jack outputs, you need a mini stereo jack to ¼" stereo jack lead.

PREPARING TO RECORD

It's a good idea to run a quick test to make sure that everything is working properly before you record your set. Otherwise you might get to the end and discover that nothing has actually been recorded!

STEP 5 STEP 4 STEP 2/3

STEP 1

1 Depending on the program you're using, you need to set up a 'monitor mix'. This allows you to hear and see the recording, so that you can monitor it. This option is usually found in one of the menus at the top — check your software manual to find it. You might have to click the record button first to then see a monitor mix check box.

2 Play some music through your mixer. If your mixer has a record level control, open it up a little. You should see a music level appearing on your recording software or hardware. (If you are using software and cannot see the recording level display, make sure that the "monitor mix" feature is selected.)

3 Set the recording levels to the correct level—just below the red level is good. If you are using hardware, you will have a recording level knob that you can adjust as necessary.

4 Now do a recording test by pressing the record button function. Play and record some music for about 10 seconds, then press stop on the recording and stop the music playing from your deck.

5 To listen back to the snippet you've recorded, press play on the software or hardware. If it sounds good, that's fantastic— you are now ready to record!

EDITING

Once you have recorded your mix, you should edit it before burning it onto a CD or creating a digital MP3 or WAV file. **Editing** just means tweaking your recording after you have finished your DJ set. It allows you to get the best possible recording for playing back.

You can edit your mix using the editing functions on your recording software. The functions that are available will depend on what recording software you are using. A basic package will have fewer editing tools than a more advanced software package.

Tip 1: CORRECT THE VOLUME

When you edit, you can adjust the overall volume level of the recording. You might want to make it louder or correct parts of the recording that may be too low or too loud. Editing gives you the opportunity to fine-tune your recording.

HANDY TIP!
If your mixer has a dedicated record out channel, you can control the recording level coming from the mixer, giving you greater control over your recording levels.

Tip 2: ADD EFFECTS

If you want, you can add effects to your recording, such as an introduction sound or voice at the beginning or end of the mix. You could also add some sounds or talking over the top of your recording.

Tip 3: NORMALIZE THE RECORDING

Normalizing is a useful feature that makes your recording the same level overall. It brings up any parts where the level is too low and matches them with the highest levels, to produce a consistent sound level.

Tip 4: TIDY IT UP

When you edit, you can get rid of any gaps, mainly at the beginning and end of the mix. But remember that whenever you do any editing, you should only do what is really necessary. Too much editing can spoil your mix!

PRODUCING A DEMO

When you have created and perfected a DJ set, recorded it, and edited it, the next step is to produce it into a demo mix. In this section, you will learn skills that will help you produce a good demo. And of course, you need to know what to do with it! If you get it right, a great demo can really make you stand out from the crowd.

WHAT IS A DEMO?

A **demo** is an audio recording that you give to someone else for promotional purposes. Back in the day we called them "demo tapes" because they were recorded onto a format called a "cassette tape." Cassettes were cheap, easily available, and easy to record onto—and that's how the demo tape was born!

These days, demos are normally recorded onto a CD or just saved and shared as a digital audio file (such as an MP3 or WAV format). No matter how you record it, your DJ demo will showcase your own unique DJ skills and style!

Tip 1: CHOOSE YOUR AUDIENCE

The whole point of a demo is to have an example of your DJing that you can pass on to other people. You may just want to share yours with your family and friends—and that's absolutely fine! But if you want to start DJing to a wider audience, you can send your demo out to people in the music industry. You might want to send your demo to music managers, record labels, clubs, radio stations, club promoters, or agents. You could even send it to other DJs or artists you admire. These people could help you advance your DJ career and get gigs and bookings.

Tip 2: PROMOTE YOURSELF

Once you have a demo recorded, you can use it to promote yourself. For example, you could create a YouTube channel and upload a video of you DJing. You could also create your own webpage or Facebook page and then upload your video or demo onto it. Social media is massive nowadays and is a great way to reach more people. SoundCloud is a good site for uploading your demos and getting your music and DJ skills out there. With luck, they'll find a wider audience!

ALWAYS ASK YOUR PARENT OR GUARDIAN FOR PERMISSION TO USE SOCIAL MEDIA. THEY WILL HELP KEEP YOU **SAFE ONLINE.**

Tip 3: KEEP IT LEGAL

You need to be aware that when you use someone else's music, you are supposed to get the creator's permission first. But this can be tricky when you are making a DJ mix with a lot of different tracks—it could take you a long time to get every song you use approved!

If you're not able to get everything approved then you need to be very careful to avoid copyright infringement issues. Instead of putting your demos online, where anyone can listen to or download them, only give them directly to contacts instead. And of course, you must not sell your mixes! It's illegal to do this, and it's also not fair, as it means that the artist who made the music in the first place won't get paid for their work and creativity.

WHAT TO INCLUDE

When producing your demo, the complete package will contain more than just the DJ mix (as either a CD or digital file). A good demo will also include the following:

- A short biography that tells people what inspires you to be a DJ and what kind of music you like. You need to sell and promote yourself, so be confident!

- A cool picture of yourself can also help. Maybe get a friend who is a good photographer to do a shoot for you!

- Social media links, such as a SoundCloud or Instagram account.

- Contact information is a must, but be careful! Don't put out private details such as your phone number or address. It is much safer to create a new email address or Facebook page, and use that as a way for people to contact you.

TAILORING YOUR DEMO

The length of your demo is totally up to you, but a mini DJ demo of 30 minutes or so is a good starting point. As you gain more experience and confidence, you can make your mixes and demos longer. You need to think about who you will be sending it to and what you want to achieve. Here are some examples of demos you could produce:

PARTY DEMO

You may want to make a demo to give to your school or local youth club. If others can hear it and like it, you might then get asked to DJ at their next youth club event!

HANDY TIP!
If you're providing social media links, make sure they are relevant and useful. Set up pages under your DJ name and link to these, not your personal pages.

RADIO DEMO

You can send a demo to an internet based radio station with the aim of getting an online radio show. When making it, think about who would be tuning in to listen to your show, and what the format of the show would be.

CLUB DEMO

As you gain more experience, you might want to make a demo to send to a club promoter. You will need to think about what kind of club it is, what kind of music style will fit, who the audience will be, and how long you would be required to play for. You also need to make sure you're the right age to play in the club, depending on what night or event it is!

Demo checklist

These are the things you should think about when putting your demo together:

- Whom do you want to hear it? Make a list of names and contacts that you want to send it to.

- Has the demo been recorded and edited nicely? Listen back to the demo to make sure that the levels are good and there are no big gaps between songs.

- Pay attention to the overall package, such as the photo and the biography. It's a good idea to ask someone older to help edit your bio, to make sure it reads well and looks great!

HANDY TIP!
Demos can often be used for more than one purpose, so always aim to make it the best you can. Be original and be yourself!!

CREATING YOUR DEMO

Once you have recorded your DJ mix and edited it, you can burn it onto a CD. You will need a CD burning software program. These are pre-loaded onto most computers. If you don't have one, you can easily download some free software, such as Windows Media Player or Express Burn.

Using these programs is really easy. Just drag and drop your DJ mix file where it says "add files to burn," then click "burn" or "record CD." When the CD is ready, it will automatically open up for you to take the CD out.

MAKING A DIGITAL DEMO

To get the best quality, record your digital demo in WAV format. This gives you a CD-quality recording with full sound, but it makes a big file. You can easily convert WAV files to MP3 files, which compress the audio file into a smaller package, making it easier to send online. However, if you use MP3 format you should record at either 256 Kbps or 320 Kbps—any lower than that and you will lose too much sound quality.

Now it's just a question of simply uploading your demo mix onto whatever platform you are using. You can also upload it to "the Cloud," an online storage system, so it will be accessible from anywhere in the world.

HANDY TIP!
You can package your DJ demo to make it attractive and appealing so that it catches people's eyes as well as their ears!

Tip 1: PAY ATTENTION TO THE COMPLETE PACKAGE

Make your demo package as good as you can! The audio recording should be clear and well-edited, but adding a short bio, a good promotional photo, and a logo can help make you stand out.

Tip 2: DO YOUR RESEARCH

A demo will only help your career if you send it to the right people. Search online to find contacts to send your demo to and make a hit list! This can include other DJs or DJ agencies, local youth clubs, radio stations, or online DJ forums. Also keep an eye out for DJ competitions—they can be a great way to get your name out there.

Tip 3: FOLLOW UP

It may take a while to get a response to your demo. If you have sent it to a local radio station and you haven't heard back after a few weeks, then give them a call or an email to follow up. Be patient but also persistent, and don't give up if you don't get a "yes" right away.

Tip 4: BE SOCIAL MEDIA SAVVY

Social media is everywhere these days, and it is a great way to connect with people all over the world. Create a Facebook page or use Snapchat or Instagram to reach out to potential fans. There are online music sites where you could upload your demo, or you could create your own website and be your own promoter!

HANDY TIP!

Never give up! Achieving success as a DJ takes persistence and belief in yourself. Keep on learning and making new demos. If you enjoy what you do, it will always show!

PLAYING LIVE

Congratulations—you've reached the final skill! It's time to tackle playing and performing live, which is what most DJs aim for. This chapter will provide tips to help you when performing live, including how to set yourself up for success and put on a great show.

WHAT PEOPLE WANT FROM A LIVE DJ

At a live performance, the crowd expects the DJ to entertain them! The DJ is the center of the event, and a good DJ will energize the crowd, who will be able to feel that energy through the music. Being a DJ is about more than just showmanship—it's about connecting with the audience so they get a great experience!

Playing live is different from playing on the radio or making a recording. When you have a live audience directly in front of you, you can see them and they can see you, making for a totally different experience.

PLAYING LIVE IS ALL ABOUT CONNECTING WITH YOUR AUDIENCE AND MAKING SURE EVERYONE HAS A GOOD TIME, INCLUDING YOU!

TYPES OF GIGS

There are many types of DJ gigs, from small events to festivals or huge stadium shows. Many DJs start their careers by playing in local bars or clubs, but there are all sorts of events where DJs are needed, such as fashion shows, weddings, and private parties. Some DJs play on the radio or on TV shows as a stepping stone to playing and touring internationally.

EXPRESS YOURSELF!

It's so important to be yourself as a DJ. The more you can express yourself through your performances, the more people will like and react to what you do. People love a cool, happy DJ with lots of energy. If you don't even look at your audience when you are playing, you will lose a sense of connection with them. But when you connect with the crowd, it creates a much better vibe. If they can see that you are enjoying yourself then they will enjoy it more too, so everybody will have more fun!

TIPS FOR SUCCESS

BE PREPARED! If you prepare your music beforehand, you will be able to relax, which makes for a better performance.

INTERACT with the crowd and make them feel welcome.

IF SOMETHING GOES WRONG, try not to worry. Life is not always perfect, and all you can do is your best.

FEEL THE MUSIC. Let the beat and vibe flow through you—not just through the speakers!

SMILE, be happy, and don't worry; everything will be alright!

ALWAYS AIM TO BE PROFESSIONAL. Expect and give the best of yourself, but don't be too hard on yourself. The crowd should have fun, and you should too!

PUTTING ON A SHOW

So this is it, this is what you have been working toward: the big show! Every gig is a show, no matter how small or big it is, so always give it your best. Here are a few tips and ideas that can help you create something really exciting and extra special!

REMEMBER THAT YOU MUST **GET PERMISSION** FROM THE VENUE BEFORE USING ANY PROPS.

Tip 1: LIGHT IT UP

Lighting really helps to add to the ambience and mood of a show. You can buy a few small portable disco lights and use them whenever you play. Some venues will have their own lighting, especially festivals, bigger clubs, and music venues. They also tend to have a lighting technician who will look after the lighting for your show.

Tip 2: USE PROPS

Using staging props can help to add to the show, but what you can use will depend on the venue and the budget. As you develop your career, stage designs and props will become more important, but there is nothing stopping you from thinking about it right from the beginning! Draw or write down any ideas—they may come in handy in the future!

Tip 3: USE DANCERS

Having some great backup dancers performing on stage with you is really cool and adds a lot of energy to your show. I trained as a professional dancer and have performed on stage with DJs and other artists, and I also like to use dancers as part of my own shows! If you have friends who are good at dancing and want to take part in your shows then go for it! Just make sure that you plan and rehearse beforehand.

HANDY TIP!
These features can support you as the DJ, but don't let them overshadow you. The music and how you play it is central to making the whole show a success.

Tip 4: PROJECT AN IMAGE

Using video projections while you DJ really adds to the mood of your set. You can project video onto the walls around you, onto a screen, or even onto the ceiling! You'll need to plan and prepare in advance so that it becomes a seamless part of the set, creating an amazing experience for the audience. Try to find someone who is good at this sort of thing to take charge of the projections while you perform, so you can concentrate on the DJing.

Tip 5: ADD AN MC

An **MC** (Master of Ceremonies) is someone who talks over a microphone, rhyming with the music and chatting to the beat. It's a form of freestyle rapping—and a skill in itself! Having a good MC who can chat or rhyme with you as you DJ can really add to your show. An MC will interact with the crowd, adding hype to a show and entertaining the audience.

GETTING READY FOR A GIG

Before you head out to a gig, you need to check that you have everything you need. There is nothing worse than turning up and realizing you have forgotten something important! Here is a checklist that will help you remember everything:

- Music prepared for your set

- Headphones to help you mix

- Laptop with controller and sound card, or CD decks/vinyl turntables with mixer

- Speakers or PA system

- Cables for connecting all your equipment together (don't forget power supply connectors and extension cables!)

- Microphone for making announcements or adding an MC

- Portable lighting

- Projection equipment, such as a video or film projector, and prepared material on a laptop

- Strong and safe flat surface to put your equipment on.

You many not have to bring all of these things to every gig, as larger venues will often have the main equipment already.

HANDY TIP!
It's a good idea to bring spares, such as spare connecting cables or needle cartridges. You never know what may need replacing in the middle of a gig!

SAFETY FIRST!

When playing at venues, you need to be aware of any safety risks. Make sure that you have the venue owner's approval before adding or bringing anything extra. You need to be aware of any safety issues that may affect your show, so be careful when planning and discuss all plans with the owner: agreement is essential on both sides.

Make sure that any equipment you bring and set up is done safely and correctly and is not hazardous to the public; for example, you do not want any speakers that you may bring to fall and hurt somebody, so make sure everything is securely and safely positioned so that nothing blocks public access and emergency exits.

READING YOUR AUDIENCE

As a DJ, you must learn to read and judge the mood of the crowd. If they don't like what you are playing, you will need to be flexible and react to this. If you see people walking away, it can be a sign that you need to change tactics and play something different. You can change the music or find another vibe that will make them happier, because there is nothing worse than playing to an empty space!

At the same time, you shouldn't forget who you are or what you stand for. Many times in the past people have come up to me during a set, asking for a certain song to be played. It may not be a song that I like, and whether I decide to play it or not is up to me! If they ask me nicely then I may well say yes, but if they are rude then maybe not! It's all about having respect on both sides.

BEING FLEXIBLE

You'll prepare your set beforehand, but being flexible also requires planning. Always have extra music with you, in case you need to change things up quickly or play for longer than expected! Keep up with the current music scene so that you are always on the pulse of what is happening. Never stop collecting music, as it is part of the love of being a DJ!

YOU ARE IN CHARGE OF YOUR SHOW. YOU ARE THE DJ. NOW GO OUT, MAKE YOUR MARK, AND LIGHT UP THE WORLD!

USEFUL LINKS

YOUTUBE LINKS:

TURNTABLE SET-UP

youtu.be/TyoZS-5yDW4

This video will give you some useful tips and information on the DJ scratch/hiphop setup.

HOW TO COUNT MUSIC (BEATS AND BARS)

youtu.be/fFcml2J5ElE

This video will give you some handy tips on how to count beats in music.

www.youtube.com/user/djTLMtv

Here you'll find plenty of tips and advice on all aspects of DJ mixing, blending, and scratching.

NOTE There are many more videos and tutorials on Youtube, so search for more information on what you need.

DJ WEBSITE LINKS:

DIGITAL DJ TIPS

www.digitaldjtips.com

Visit this website for some great advice on digital DJ equipment.

kwotemusic.com/scratchdjtechnique.html

Here you'll find a list of different scratches and videos demonstrating their uses.

ONLINE STORE LINKS:

Here are a few websites where you can purchase vinyl records and DJ equipment. There are many more websites, so do search further online.

JUNO RECORDS

www.juno.co.uk

HARD TO FIND RECORDS

www.htfr.com

RUBADUB MUSIC AND TECHNOLOGY

www.rubadub.co.uk

DJ PLANET.COM

www.planetdj.com/dj-equipment

GEAR 4 MUSIC

www.gear4music.com

EDUCATION LINKS:

DJ SCHOOL UK

djschooluk.org.uk

DJ School UK is a DJ academy based in Leeds, UK.

BDJ

www.facebook.com/djboomadjworkshops

Here you'll find workshops, videos, and tips from the author of this book, DJ Booma.

DJ WORKSHOP DEMONSTRATION

www.youtube.com/watch?v=TBgztBW01jg

A video from an international youth exchange DJ workshop, delivered by DJ Booma in Denmark, demonstrating beat counting and scratches.

Website information is correct at time of going to press. The publishers cannot accept liability for any information or links found on third party websites.

GLOSSARY

A CAPPELLA singing or rapping without musical accompaniment

ACTIVE SPEAKER loudspeaker with a built-in amplifier

ANALOG continuous signal used by older equipment, such as vinyl decks

BAR segments of music containing beats which are repeated throughout a track

BEAT pulse of a piece of music. DJs count beats in fours or eights to mix it

BPM beats per minute in a song

CROSS FADER switch on a DJ mixer which allows the DJ to start, stop, or switch sounds faster

CUE POINT marking a specific point on a piece of music

DECK piece of hardware used for playing CDs or Vinyl with the intention of mixing them

DEMO recording of a mix used to promote a DJ's skills

DIGITAL newer type of signal expressed by the digits 1 and 0

DJ MIXER piece of equipment that allows a DJ to mix different music together

EDITING altering and correcting a piece of recorded music to produce a final mix

EQ BUTTONS allow the DJ to alter the frequencies in the music

INPUT CHANNEL path through which information travels from a piece of hardware into a computer

LOOP when a small section of music is set to play on repeat

MIX when a DJ takes two or more pieces of music and blends them together

MONO when sound is emitted from the same area, giving a smaller and less direct sound

MP3 audio format where a sound sequence is compressed into a very small file for digital storage

MP4 digital multimedia format commonly used to store audio and video files

OUTPUT CHANNEL path through which information travels from a computer to a piece of hardware

RPM revolutions (spins or turns) per minute

SAMPLE sound which is taken from another song and used in a mix to create something new

SCRATCHING when a DJ takes one sound and plays it repeatedly over another piece of music

SOUND CARD equipment that changes digital music files into audio signals so that you can hear the music

STEREO when sound is emitted from different areas which creates a wider and more direct sound

TRADEMARK clear, unique, and distinctive sound, sign, or style that clearly indentifies something or someone

TURNTABLE record deck that plays vinyl records specifically designed for DJing

VINYL also known as a record, contains analog signals cut into the grooves which form a track

VOLUME FADERS sliders that allow the DJ to mix music from two different decks

WAV audio file format used for storing uncompressed audio files on PCs

WAVEFORM visual shape formation of a signal

INDEX

a cappella vocals 33
apps 13
Audacity software 45

baby scratch 31
backup dancers 59
bars 16, 20, 21
  loops 20
'battles' 29
beats 16–17
  bars 16, 20, 21
  on beat 17
  beat juggling 28
  beat matching/mixing 22, 25,
  35, 36, 37
  counting 18–19
  finding the beat 19, 21
  off beat 17
breakdancing 28, 29
burning software 54

cables 5, 14
CD decks 5, 10, 15, 41
  features 10
CD recorders 46
club demos 53
club DJs 9
controllers 5, 12, 13, 15
copyright infringement issues 51
courses 9
Cox, Carl 7
cue points 40–42
cutting 32–33

decks see CD decks; vinyl decks
demos 50–55
  burning 54
  club demo 53
  contact information 52
  DJ biography and picture 52, 53
  follow up 55
  legal issues 51
  length of 52
  packaging 53, 54
  party demo 52
  radio demo 53
  self-promotion 51
  social media links 52, 55
  uploading 51, 54
  WAV format 54
  who to send to 52, 53, 55
DJ Kool Herc 6
DJ sets
  cue points 40–42

links 39
mini DJ set 43
mood 40
opening 39
planning and preparation 38–43
recording a set 44–49
DJs
  expressing yourself 57
  famous DJs 6, 7
  first DJs 6–7
  types of 9
  watching and listening to 7, 8
  what DJ means 7

editing a mix 48–49
equipment 10–15
  apps 13
  choosing and buying 14
  controllers 5, 12, 13, 15
  decks see CD decks; vinyl decks
  hardware 5, 10–11
  headphones 5, 12, 14, 15
  mixers 5, 12, 15, 30
  safety 14
  setup 15
  software 5, 12–13
  sound cards 5, 13
  speakers 5, 12, 15

faders/cross faders 12, 30, 31,
  32, 33
forward scratch (cutting) 32–33

hand claps 18, 19
hardware 5, 10–11
  recording hardware 46–47
  setup 15
headphones 5, 12, 14, 15
hip-hop 6, 9, 17, 28, 31
hip-hop DJs 9, 28, 33
house DJs 9
house music 9, 17

laptops 5, 13, 15
lighting 58
links 39
live performance see playing live

MCs 59
mixers 5, 12, 15, 30
  features 12
mixing 6, 17, 22–27
  beat matching/mixing 22, 25,
  35, 36, 37

blend mixing 24, 34
combining mixing and scratching
37
cutting (dropping) in the mix
26, 27
good and bad mixes 27
remixes 9
techniques 24–26
mood 40
MP3 files 54
MP3 recorders 46
music collection 8

normalizing 49

online music sites 8, 55

party demos 52
phono-to-phono leads 46
phrases 16
pitch control 10, 11, 35
playing live 56–61
  backup dancers 59
  checklist 60
  connecting with your audience
  57, 61
  flexibility 61
  gigs 57
  lighting 58
  MCs 59
  props 58
  safety 61
  top tips 57
  video projections 59
practice 9, 34–37
props 58

radio demos 53
radio DJs 9
rap 9
recording a DJ set 44–49
  balance (PAN) 44
  connecting recording devices 46
  demos 50–55
  editing 48–49
  effects, adding 49
  hardware 46–47
  mono recording 44
  normalizing 49
  recording levels 47, 49
  setting up for recording 47
  software 45
  stereo recording 44
  test recording 48

remixers 9
reverse scratch 33
rhythm 16, 18, 21, 28
  see also beats

safety 14
  playing live 61
scratching 28–33
  baby scratch 31
  'battles' 29
  combining mixing and scratching
  37
  forward scratch (cutting) 32–33
  reverse scratch 33
  scribble (wobble) scratch 33
scribble (wobble) scratch 33
self-promotion 51
social media 51, 52, 55
software 5, 12–13
  burning software 54
  editing tools 48
  recording software 45
  setup 15
sound cards 5, 13
Sound Forge software 45
soundbites 39
SoundCloud 51
speakers 5, 12, 15
  active/passive 12

Technics 1210 7
tempo 25
Tong, Pete 7
tools see equipment
turntables see vinyl decks
turntablism 6, 28
tutorials, online 8, 9, 29, 31

video projections 59
vinyl decks 5, 6, 7, 11, 15, 41
  belt driven 11
  direct drive 11
  features 11
vinyl records 8, 11, 19
  scratching 28–33

WAV format 54
waveforms 13, 36–37
writing down music (notation) 18

YouTube videos 8, 51